Popular Teaching Resources

Quick Math
Assessments

Grade 6

Table of Contents

Number Sense and Numeration

Large Numbers

writing large numbers in different forms and comparing, ordering, and rounding them

Write the numbers in the place-value chart. Then order them and write them in different forms.

1.

A 31 246 539

B 4.5 million

C $14\frac{3}{4}$ million

Millions			Thousands			Units		
H	T	O	H	T	O	H	T	O
								9

2. greatest to least: _____

3. Write the numbers in words and in expanded form.

A _____

  _____

B _____

  _____

C _____

  _____

Round each number to the nearest million, hundred thousand, and ten thousand.

4. 36 543 651   _____   _____   _____

5. 10 653 462   _____   _____   _____

Common Multiple

finding the common multiples of a set of numbers

Mark the multiples of the numbers. Then fill in the blanks.

1.

1	2	3	4	5	6	7	8	9	10
11	12	13	14	15	16	17	18	19	20
21	22	23	24	25	26	27	28	29	30

☆ – multiples of 2

◯ – multiples of 3

2. common multiples of 2 and 3: _____

(the numbers marked "☆") _____

3. the least common multiple of 2 and 3: _____

List the first 6 multiples of each pair of numbers. Then find their common multiples and the least common multiple (L.C.M.).

4. **4**: _____ , _____ , _____ , _____ , _____ , _____
     1 x 4   2 x 4   3 x 4   4 x 4   5 x 4   6 x 4

    6: _____ , _____ , _____ , _____ , _____ , _____
     1 x 6   2 x 6   3 x 6   4 x 6   5 x 6   6 x 6

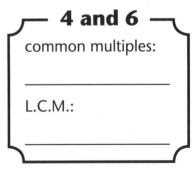

— **4 and 6** —
common multiples:
_____

L.C.M.:
_____

5. **5**: _____ , _____ , _____ , _____ , _____ , _____
     1 x 5   2 x 5   3 x 5   4 x 5   5 x 5   6 x 5

    10: _____ , _____ , _____ , _____ , _____ , _____
     1 x 10   2 x 10   3 x 10   4 x 10   5 x 10   6 x 10

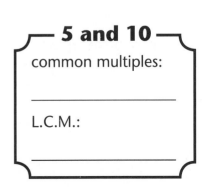

— **5 and 10** —
common multiples:
_____

L.C.M.:
_____

Prime and Composite Numbers

identifying numbers as prime or composite numbers

Fill in the blanks. List out all the factors of each number. Then tell whether it is a prime or composite number.

1. **Prime Number**: a number with only ____ factors (1 and itself)

    e.g.   The factors of 5: 1 and 5

    So, 5 is a prime number.

    Composite Number: a number with more than ____ factors

    e.g.   The factors of 4: 1, 2, and 4

    So, 4 is a composite number.

2. The factors of 42:

    _____

    42 : a _____ number

3. The factors of 20:

    _____

    20 : a _____ number

4. The factors of 19:

    _____

    19 : a _____ number

5. The factors of 9:

    _____

    9 : a _____ number

Write the numbers.

6. 2 prime numbers that are between 15 and 20   _____

7. 2 composite numbers that are greater than 20   _____

8. a prime number that is an even number   _____

                        Quick Math Assessments | G.6

Integers

using integers to describe different situations

Write the missing integers. Then write "positive" or "negative" in the boxes and fill in the blanks.

1.

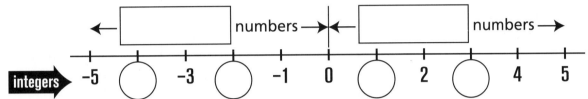

2. _____ numbers are always shown with a minus sign (–). They are to

the _____ (left / right) of 0 on a horizontal number line.

3. _____ numbers may or may not be shown with a plus sign (+). They

are to the _____ (left / right) of 0 on a horizontal number line.

Write an integer to describe each situation.

4.   Judy's dog gained 2 kg this year.   _____

5.   Leon has saved $15 this month.   _____

6.   The temperature is 30°C below 0°C.   _____

7.   The basketball team lost 4 points.   _____

Write a situation that describes the given integer.

8.   +10 cm   _____

9.   -3 L   _____

10. -$12   _____

Order of Operations

following the order of operations to solve expressions

Follow the order of operations to find the answers. Circle the parts to be done first.

── Solving an Expression

1st	Do the operations in brackets.
2nd	Do "x" or "÷" in order from left to right.
3rd	Do "+" or "−" in order from left to right.

Do "x" first.

e.g. $16 - \boxed{2 \times 3}$

$= 16 - 6$

$= \underline{10}$

Do the part inside the brackets first.

e.g. $\boxed{(16 - 2)} \times 3$

$= 14 \times 3$

$= \underline{42}$

---

1. $34 - \boxed{12 \div 3}$

$= \underline{34 - 4}$

$= \underline{30}$

2. $9 + 5 \times 2$

$= \underline{9 + 10}$

$= \underline{19}$

3. $(2 + 3) \times 6$

$= \underline{5 \times 6}$

$= \underline{30}$

4. $18 + 6 \div 2$

$= \underline{18 + 3}$

$= \underline{21}$

5. $5 \times 6 \div 3$

$= \underline{30 \div 3}$

$= \underline{10}$

6. $9 \times (8 - 3)$

$= \underline{9 \times 5}$

$= \underline{45}$

7. $52 + 6 \times 7 = \underline{52 + 42}$

$= \underline{94}$

8. $26 - 14 \div 2 = \underline{26 - 7}$

$= \underline{9}$

Add brackets to make each number sentence true.

9. $(36 + 3) \div 3 = 13$

10. $7 \times (2 + 1) = 21$

Addition and Subtraction

adding and subtracting whole numbers

Round each number to the nearest hundred to estimate each sum. Then find the exact answer.

1.

```
   OO
  2 2 4        ┌─ Estimate ─
  4 7 5        │   2 0 0
  3 9 2        │
+ 7 1 8        │ +
```

2.
```
   OO
  3 2 1        ┌─ Estimate ─
  2 1 9        │   3 0 0
  3 5 6        │
+ 1 4 2        │ +
```

Subtract. Then use addition to check the answers.

3.
```
  1 3 8 2 4
  –   7 9 6 6
  ┌─────────┐
  │         │
  └─────────┘
```
Add these two numbers. If the sum is 13 824, it means you did the subtraction correctly; otherwise, you need to do the subtraction again.

Check
```
┌─────────┐
│         │
└─────────┘
+   7 9 6 6
┌─────────┐
│         │
└─────────┘
```

4.
```
  4 5 2 0 8
– 1 3 6 4 5
```

Check

5.
```
  6 4 5 2 9
– 1 8 7 2 6
```

Check

6.
```
  3 8 5 6 2
– 1 5 3 7 1
```
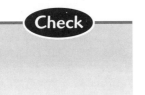
Check

7.
```
  9 4 2 5 8
– 3 6 2 8 8
```

Check

Multiplication

multiplying 3-digit numbers by 2-digit numbers

Do the multiplication. Then solve the problem.

1.
```
      2 2 1
  x     6 7
```
[ ][ ][ ][ ] ← 7 x 221
[ ][ ][ ][ ] ← 60 x 221
[ ][ ][ ][ ][ ]

2.
```
      4 7 2
  x     2 9
```
[ ][ ][ ][ ] ← 9 x 472
[ ][ ][ ][ ] ← 20 x 472
[ ][ ][ ][ ][ ]

3.
```
      7 6 2
  x     5 8
```

4.
```
      3 5 8
  x     6 1
```

5.
```
      8 4 4
  x     3 5
```

6. Each box contains 255 batteries. How many batteries do 16 boxes hold in all?

4080

Estimate to check whether each product is "reasonable" or "unreasonable".

7. 649 x 52 = _23748_ (   )

8. 324 x 67 = _21708_ (   )

9. 162 x 89 = _14418_ (   )

           Quick Math Assessments | G.6

Division

dividing 4-digit numbers by 2-digit numbers

Do the division. Then check the answers.

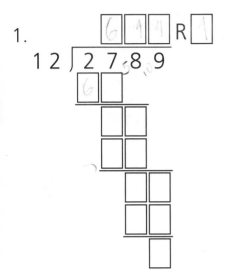

1.

Steps to Check Answers

1st quotient x divisor

2nd answer from **1st** + remainder

If the answer got in **2nd** is the same as the dividend, it means you did the division correctly; otherwise, you need to do the division again.

Check

1st _____ x _____ = _____
       quotient   divisor

2nd _____ + _____ = _____
    from **1st**   remainder   (should be equal to 2789)

2. **A**   38) 7 2 3 5

B   19) 8 0 3 2

C   15) 6 0 8 3

D   92) 1 6 5 3

Check

A _____ x _____ = _____

_____ + _____ = _____

B

C

D

Decimals

writing decimals to thousandths

Write a decimal to describe the shaded blocks. Then write it in expanded form and in words.

1.

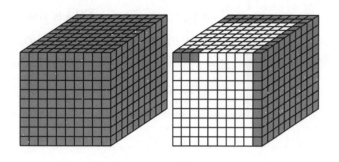

In numeral: _____

In expanded form: _____

In words: _____

Writing Decimals

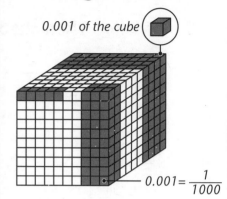

0.001 of the cube

$0.001 = \frac{1}{1000}$

0.465 (four hundred sixty-five thousandths) of the cube is shaded.

In expanded form:

$0.465 = 0.4 + 0.06 + 0.005$

Write each in 2 different forms.

2. two and sixty-five thousandths

_____

3. $10 + 5 + 0.6 + 0.008$

_____

4. $400 + 3 + 0.07 + 0.009$

_____

5. 3.254

_____

Decimals

comparing, ordering, and rounding decimals

Round each decimal to the nearest hundredth. Draw arrows to locate the decimals on the number line. Then order them.

1.

	rounded to
24.187	_24.19_
24.122	_____
24.156	_____

least to greatest: _____

2.

	rounded to
36.318	_____
36.381	_____
36.345	_____

greatest to least: _____

Put the decimals in order from least to greatest. Then write the decimal that is one thousandth greater than the greatest decimal in each group.

the greatest

3. 4.365   3.465   4.635   3.654

In order: _____

4. 12.008   2.008   8.012   2.081

In order: _____

Name: _____   Date: _____

Adding and Subtracting Decimals

adding and subtracting decimals to thousandths

Don't forget to align the decimal points when you add or subtract.

Find the answers.

1.
```
   align
    ↓  ① ①
   2.6 8 9
 + 1.2 4 8
  _____
   3.9 3 7
```

2.
```
    align
  ① ↓ ① ①
   4.3 7 9
 + 5.8 9 3
  _____
  1 0.2 7 2
```

3.
```
   align
    ↓
   9.6 5 1
 - 3.9 6 7
  _____
  □.□ □ □
```

4.

6.25 and 3.273	
Sum	**Difference**

```
      place holder              place holder
         ↓                         ↓
   6.2 5 0                   6.2 5 0
 + 3.2 7 3                 - 3.2 7 3
  _____              _____
```

5.

7.5 and 3.277	
Sum	**Difference**

```
 + _____            - _____
```

6.

0.375 L   2.5 L

a. How much juice is there in all?

b. How much more juice is there in the carton than in the box?

7.

2.885 m

Mr. Cowen cuts the rope into 2 pieces. If one piece is 1.57 m long, how long is the other?

                        Quick Math Assessments | G.6

Multiplying Decimals

multiplying decimals by whole numbers, 10, 100, 1000, or 10 000 and multiplying decimals by 0.1, 0.01, or 0.001

Decimals x Whole Numbers

decimal ◄┐
x whole number   ├ *They have the same number*
decimal ◄┘   *of decimal places.*

Do the multiplication.

1.　　 8 . 2 9 4 ◄ *3 decimal places*
　　 x 　　　 7
　　 ☐☐.☐☐☐ ◄ *3 decimal places*

2.　 1 2.6 5 3
　　 x 　　 9

3.　　 8.7 6 4
　　 x 　　 8

4.　　 9.5 0 7
　　 x 　　 5

Draw arrows to show how to move the decimal points to find the answers.

Move the Decimal Point

x 10:　 **1** place to the right
x 100:　 **2** places to the right
x 1000:　 **3** places to the right
x 10 000:　 **4** places to the right

Move the Decimal Point

x 0.1:　 **1** place to the left
x 0.01:　 **2** places to the left
x 0.001:　 **3** places to the left

5.　 4.27 x 100　 = _____

6.　 20.314 x 10　 = _____

7.　 1.74 x 10 000 = _____

8.　 0.07 x 1000　 = _____

9.　 20.61 x 0.01　 = _____

10.　 125.3 x 0.001 = _____

11.　 1.5 x 0.1　　 = _____

12.　 0.18 x 0.001　 = _____

Dividing Decimals

dividing decimals by 1-digit numbers or by 0.1, 0.01, and 0.001

Do the division.

— Steps to Do Division —

1st   Divide as we do division with whole numbers.

2nd   Put the decimal point in the quotient directly above the one in the dividend.

1.

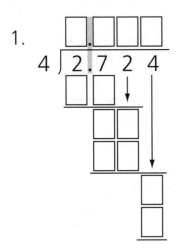

A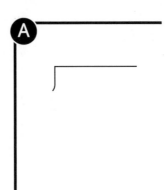

B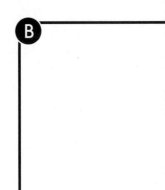

2.   **A** $5.976 \div 3 \ = \ $ _____

     B $7.476 \div 7 \ = \ $ _____

     C $8.936 \div 8 \ = \ $ _____

     D $12.264 \div 6 = $ _____

C   **D**

Draw arrows to show how to move the decimal points to find the answers.

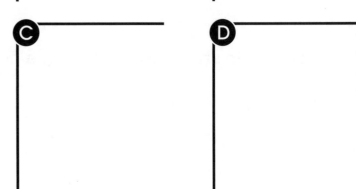

— Move the Decimal Point —

   $\div\ 0.1$: **1** place to the right

   $\div\ 0.01$: **2** places to the right

   $\div\ 0.001$: **3** places to the right

   e.g.

       $472.35 \div 0.01 = \underline{47\ 235}$

3. $125.84 \div 0.1 \ \ = \ $ _____

4. $20.94 \div 0.01 \ \ = \ $ _____

5. $3.654 \div 0.1 \ \ = \ $ _____

6. $28.204 \div 0.001 = \ $ _____

Fractions

finding equivalent fractions and writing fractions in simplest form

Find two equivalent fractions – one by multiplication and one by division. Write the fraction in simplest form in the box.

— Finding Equivalent Fractions —

By Multiplication:

multiply the denominator and the numerator by the same number

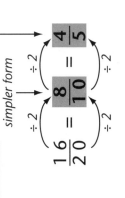

$$\frac{16}{20} = \frac{48}{60} \quad (\times 3)$$

By Division:

divide the denominator and the numerator by the same number

$$\frac{16}{20} = \frac{8}{10} = \frac{4}{5}$$

$\div 2 \qquad \div 2$

simpler form   simplest form

$$\frac{16}{20}, \frac{48}{60}, \frac{8}{10}, \text{ and } \frac{4}{5} \text{ are equivalent fractions.}$$

simplest form: the common factor of the denominator and the numerator of a fraction is 1 only

1. $\dfrac{18}{20}$ ⬜ _____

2. $\dfrac{10}{15}$ ⬜ _____

3. $\dfrac{48}{50}$ ⬜ _____

4. $\dfrac{12}{18}$ ⬜ _____

5. $\dfrac{16}{24}$ ⬜ _____

6. $\dfrac{24}{30}$ ⬜ _____

Put the fractions in order from least to greatest.

7. $\dfrac{4}{5}, \dfrac{17}{20}, \dfrac{9}{10}$ _____

8. $\dfrac{2}{5}, \dfrac{1}{4}, \dfrac{3}{20}$ _____

9. $\dfrac{4}{7}, \dfrac{1}{3}, \dfrac{16}{21}$ _____

10. $\dfrac{5}{6}, \dfrac{11}{18}, \dfrac{2}{3}$ _____

Adding and Subtracting Fractions

adding and subtracting fractions with the same denominators

Adding and Subtracting

Fractions with Same Denominators

1st Add or subtract the numerators.

2nd Keep the denominators.

3rd Write the answers in simplest form.

Colour the diagrams to match the fractions. Then find the answers.

1. $\dfrac{5}{12}$ + $\dfrac{4}{12}$ = $\dfrac{}{12}$ = $\dfrac{}{4}$

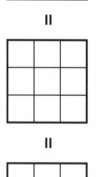

2. $\dfrac{7}{9}$ − $\dfrac{1}{9}$ = $\dfrac{}{9}$ = $\dfrac{}{3}$

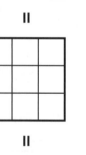

Add or subtract. Write the answers in simplest form.

3. $\dfrac{8}{16}$ − $\dfrac{4}{16}$ = $\dfrac{}{16}$ = ____

4. $\dfrac{9}{10}$ − $\dfrac{4}{10}$ = ____ = ____

5. $\dfrac{3}{12}$ + $\dfrac{9}{12}$ = $\dfrac{}{12}$ = ____

6. $\dfrac{1}{8}$ + $\dfrac{1}{8}$ = ____ = ____

7. $\dfrac{4}{15}$ + $\dfrac{6}{15}$ = $\dfrac{}{15}$ = ____

8. $\dfrac{5}{6}$ − $\dfrac{1}{6}$ = ____ = ____

9. $\dfrac{8}{9}$ − $\dfrac{5}{9}$ = $\dfrac{}{9}$ = ____

10. $\dfrac{3}{10}$ + $\dfrac{5}{10}$ = ____ = ____

Percent

relating fractions, decimals, and percents and finding a percent of a number

Write each as a fraction, a decimal, or a percent.

1. $\dfrac{45}{100}$ _____ _____

2. 82% _____ _____

3. 0.54 _____ _____

4. $\dfrac{9}{100}$ _____ _____

5. 36% _____ _____

6. 0.7 _____ _____

Find the amounts. Show your work.

— Finding a Percent of a Number

Way 1: using equivalent fractions

20% of 50

Think: 20% = $\dfrac{\boxed{}}{100}$ = $\dfrac{\boxed{}}{10}$ = $\dfrac{\boxed{}}{50}$ (× 5)   (× 5)

So, 20% of 50 = _____

We may use either way to find the amounts.

Way 2: using multiplication

20% of 50

Think: 20% = $\dfrac{\boxed{}}{100}$ = $\dfrac{\boxed{}}{50}$

$\dfrac{1}{10}$ of 50 = $\dfrac{50}{10}$ = _____

$\dfrac{2}{10}$ of 50 = 2 × _____ = _____

So, 20% of 50 = _____

7. 30% of 50

= _____

8. 5% of 20

= _____

9. 40% of 40

= _____

Ratio

comparing figures using ratio

Look at each group of pictures. Write the ratios.

1.

2.

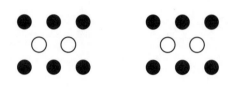

a.   Boys to Girls = _3 : 5_

b.   Girls to All = _5 : 8_

c.   Boys to All = _3 : 8_

a.   ● to ○ = _12 : 4_

b.   ● to All = _12 : 16_

c.   All to ○ = _16 : 4_

3.

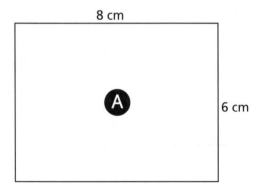

8 cm

A

6 cm

3 cm

B

2 cm

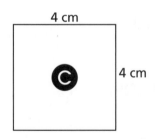

4 cm

C

4 cm

a.   Perimeter of **A** : Perimeter of **B** = _48 : 6_

b.   Perimeter of **A** : Perimeter of **C** = _48 : 16_

c.   Area of **B** : Area of **C** = _____

d.   Area of **C** : Area of **A** = _____

Rate

writing amounts as rates and comparing rates

Write each amount as a rate.

1. 6 boxes of cereal cost $13.44.

   _____

2. There are 96 sausages on 8 plates.

   _____

3. Judy completed 16 assignments in 4 days.   _____

4. Mr. Jenkins gives 108 stickers to 12 children.   _____

5. Sam types 156 words in 2 minutes.   _____

Complete the tables and the graph. Then fill in the blanks.

6. Julie makes 15 necklaces in 2 hours and Susan makes 12 in 1.5 hours.

   a.

Time (h)	2	4	6
Julie	18		

Time (h)	1.5	3	4.5
Susan	15		

   b. _____ has a higher rate.

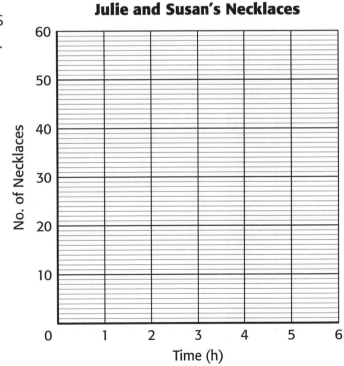

Julie and Susan's Necklaces

(graph: No. of Necklaces vs Time (h), y-axis 0–60, x-axis 0–6)

Number Sense and Numeration

Skills	Level			
	1	2	3	4
represent, compare, and order whole numbers to 1 000 000				
multiply and divide whole numbers by 2-digit numbers				
multiply whole numbers by 0.1, 0.01, and 0.001				
solve problems involving whole numbers to one million using different operations				
identify integers and use them in real life situations				
identify prime numbers and composite numbers				
represent, compare, and order decimals to 0.001				
add and subtract decimals to 0.001				
multiply and divide decimals to tenth by 10, 100, 1000, and 10 000 and by 1-digit numbers				
solve problems using the correct order of operations				
represent, compare, and order fractions with unlike denominators, including proper and improper fractions and mixed numbers				
add and subtract fractions				
relate decimals, fractions, and percents				
write ratios and equivalent ratios				
find rates and unit rates				

Level 1 – Student shows little or no understanding of the concept and is rarely able to apply the required skills.

Level 2 – Student shows some understanding of the concept and is sometimes able to apply the required skills.

Level 3 – Student shows a good understanding of the concept and is usually able to apply the required skills.

Level 4 – Student shows an excellent understanding of the concept and is consistently able to apply the required skills.

Comments: _____

Measurement

Time, Distance, and Average Speed

relating time, distance, and average speed

Average Speed

= distance ÷ time

Find the average speed of each means of transport. Then answer the questions.

1. **Travel 452 km in 2 h.**

   average speed

   = _____ ÷ _____

   = _____ (km/h)

2. **Travel 564 km in 3 h.**

   average speed

   = _____ ÷ _____

   = _____ (km/h)

3. **Travel 326 km in 2 h.**

   average speed

   = _____ ÷ _____

   = _____ (km/h)

4. **Travel 260 km in 4 h.**

   average speed

   = _____ ÷ _____

   = _____ (km/h)

5. Which means of transport has the highest speed?

   _____

6. Complete the table to show the distance travelled by the means of transport with the highest speed.

   a. **Distance Travelled**

Time (h)	Distance (km)
1	
2	
3	
4	
5	

   b. How far does it go in 6 hours?

   _____

Area of a Parallelogram

finding areas of parallelograms using a formula

Trace the correct dotted line to show the height of each parallelogram. Then find its area.

1.
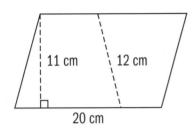

11 cm   12 cm

20 cm

Area = _____ x _____

= _____ (cm²)

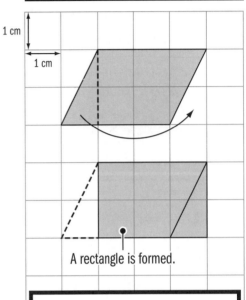

A rectangle is formed.

Area of the parallelogram
= Area of the rectangle
= 3 x 2
= 6 (cm²)

2.
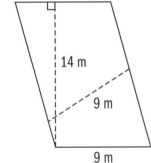

14 m

9 m

9 m

Area = _____

= _____

3.

A
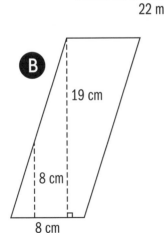

17 m

18 m

22 m

Area

B

19 cm

8 cm

8 cm

C

40 cm

32 cm

21 cm

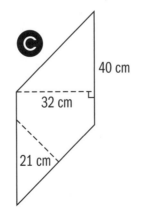

A : _____

= _____

B : _____

= _____

C : _____

= _____

Area of a Triangle

finding areas of triangles using a formula

Complete the formula for finding the area of a triangle. Draw and measure the height of each triangle. Then apply the formula to find the area of each triangle with the given base.

1.

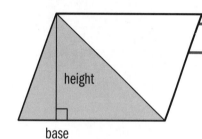

height

base

A parallelogram can be formed by 2 congruent triangles.

Area of a triangle = Area of a parallelogram ÷ 2

= _____ x _____ ÷ 2

2.

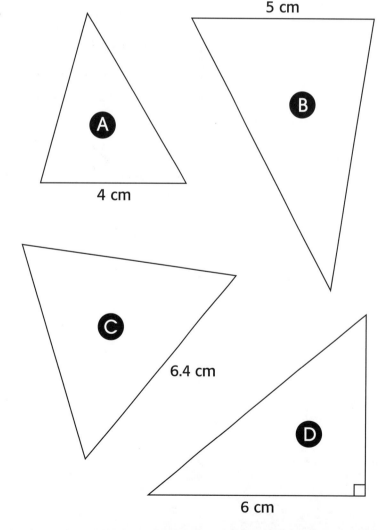

5 cm

4 cm

6.4 cm

6 cm

Area

A : _____ x _____ ÷ 2

= _____ (cm²)

B : _____

= _____ (cm²)

C : _____

= _____ (cm²)

D : _____

= _____ (cm²)

Surface Area of a Rectangular Prism

finding surface areas of rectangular prisms using nets

Colour each pair of congruent faces with the specified colour. Label the dimensions. Then find the surface area of the rectangular prism.

1.

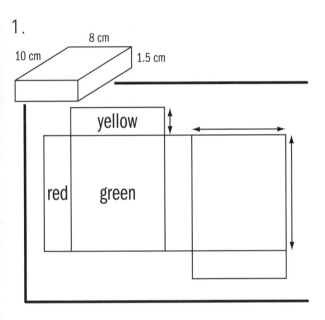

Area

2 green rectangles: _____ x _____ x 2

= _____ (cm²)

2 red rectangles: _____

= _____ (cm²)

2 yellow rectangles: _____

= _____ (cm²)

Surface area of the rectangular prism: _____ + _____ + _____

= _____ (cm²)

Find the surface area of each rectangular prism.

2.

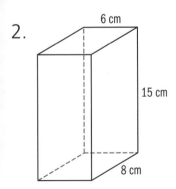

3.

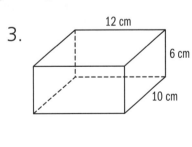

Surface Area of a Rectangular Prism

solving problems related to surface areas of rectangular prisms

Find the surface area (S.A.) of each gift box. Then match the gift box with the appropriate wrapping paper. Write the letter.

1.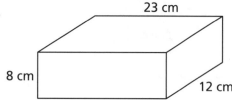

   S.A.: _____ cm²

   Wrapping paper: _____

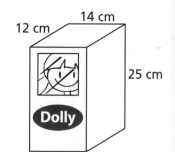

2.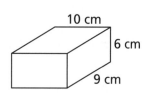

   S.A.: _____

   Wrapping paper: _____

3.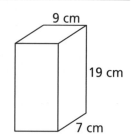

   S.A.: _____

   Wrapping paper: _____

Solve the problems.

4. How much wrapping paper is needed to wrap the box?

   _____

5. If Jane wraps 2 boxes side by side, how much wrapping paper does she need?

   _____

Surface Area of a Triangular Prism

finding surface areas of triangular prisms using a formula

Surface Area of a Triangular Prism

$$= \text{Area of 2 triangular faces} + \text{Area of 3 rectangular faces}$$

Find the surface area of each triangular prism.

1.

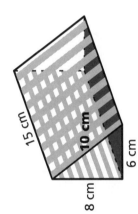

Area of 2 triangular faces

$$= \underline{}_{\text{base}} \times \underline{}_{\text{height}} \div 2 \times 2$$

$$= \underline{}$$

$$= \underline{} \, (cm^2)$$

Area of 3 rectangular faces

$$= \underline{} \times \underline{} + \underline{} \times \underline{} + \underline{} \times \underline{}$$

$$= \underline{}$$

$$= \underline{} \, (cm^2)$$

Surface area of the triangular prism: $\underline{} + \underline{} = \underline{} \, (cm^2)$

2.

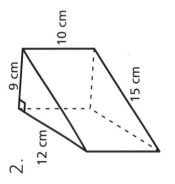

3.

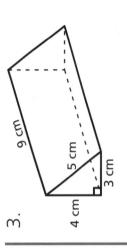

Surface Area and Volume

finding and comparing surface areas and volumes of rectangular prisms

Find the surface area and volume of each rectangular prism. Then answer the questions.

1.

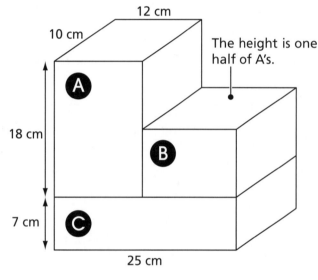

Volume of a Rectangular Prism

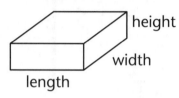

Volume = length x width x height

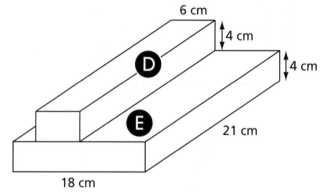

A   Surface area: Volume:

B   Surface area: Volume:

C Surface area: Volume:

D Surface area: Volume:

E Surface area: Volume:

2. Which prism has the greatest surface area?   _____

3. Which prism has the greatest volume?   _____

4. Does the prism that has the greatest surface area also
   have the greatest volume?   _____

5. If **E** is cut into 2 rectangular prisms and one of them has the same dimensions
   as **D**, what will the surface area and volume of the other rectangular prism
   be?

   _____

Volume of a Triangular Prism

relating volumes of rectangular prisms and triangular prisms

Find the volume of each triangular prism.

── Volume of a Triangular Prism ──

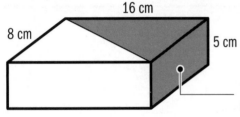

Volume of a triangular prism $=$ Volume of a rectangular prism $\div$ 2

Volume of the shaded triangular prism $= (16 \times 8 \times 5) \div 2 = \underline{320\ (cm^2)}$

1.

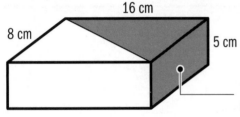

Volume

$=$

4.

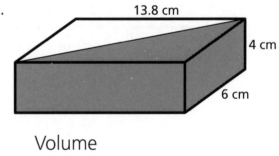

Volume

$=$

2.

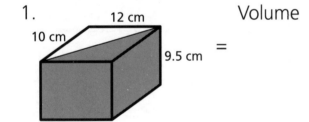

Volume

$=$

5.

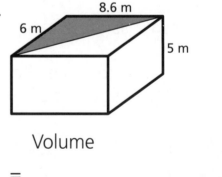

Volume

$=$

3.

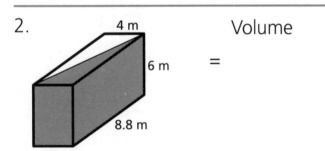

Volume

$=$

Volume of a Rectangular Prism

solving problems related to rectangular prisms

Complete the table. Then answer the questions.

1.

Rectangular Prism	Length	Width	Height	Volume
A	16 cm	8 cm		640 cm³
B		9 cm	7 cm	819 cm³
C	14 cm		3 cm	302.4 cm³
D		6 cm	9 cm	572.4 cm³

2. Jason removes a small rectangular prism from A. What is the volume of this solid?

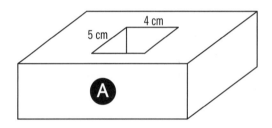

_____

3. Katie forms a letter "T" with C and another rectangular prism E. What is the volume of letter "T"?

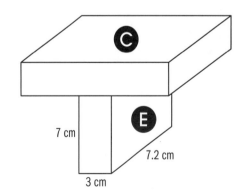

_____

Unit Conversions

converting between units of volume and capacity

Use the relationships between units of volume and capacity to do the conversions.

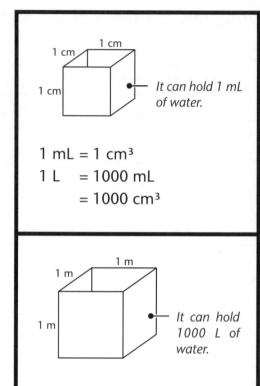

It can hold 1 mL of water.

1 mL = 1 cm³
1 L = 1000 mL
     = 1000 cm³

It can hold 1000 L of water.

1 m³ = 1000 L
1 m³ = 1000 x 1000 cm³
     = 1 000 000 cm³

1. 5400 mL   = _____ cm³

              = _____ L

2. 46 500 mL   = _____ cm³

              = _____ L

3. 390 cm³   = _____ mL

              = _____ L

4. 86 cm³   = _____ mL

              = _____ L

5. 68 000 L   = _____ m³

              = _____ cm³

6. 495 000 cm³ = _____ L

              = _____ m³

7. 875 L   = _____ m³

            = _____ cm³

8. 0.54 m³ = _____ L

          = _____ cm³

Name: _____   Date: _____

Volume and Capacity

solving problems related to the unit conversions of volume and capacity

Solve the problems.

1. How many litres of water can the water tank hold?

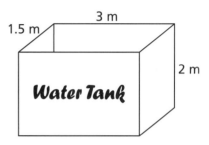

_____

2. If 450 000 cm³ of metal blocks are put into the water tank, how many litres of water can the water tank hold now?

_____

3. The water tank is half-filled with water. If Jason uses a box measuring 8 cm by 10 cm by 5 cm to remove the water from the tank, how many times does Jason need to empty the box to have the job done?

_____

4. If the length, width, and height of the water tank double, how many litres of water can the new water tank hold?

_____

Volume and Capacity of a Rectangular Prism

solving problems related to volume and capacity of rectangular prisms

Find the volume of each container and write the capacity in litres. Then answer the questions.

1.

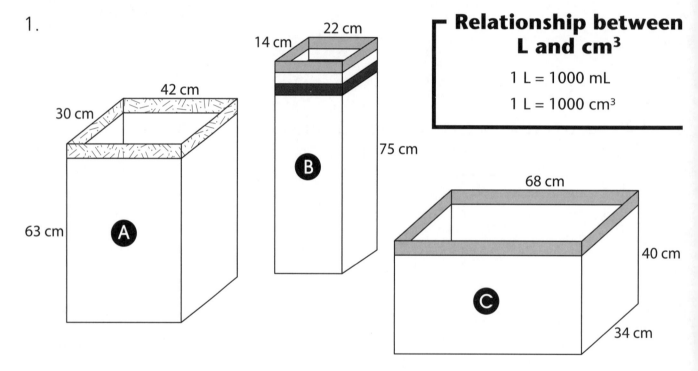

Relationship between L and cm³

1 L = 1000 mL

1 L = 1000 cm³

Ⓐ Volume: _____ x _____ x _____ = _____ (cm³)
           length   width   height

Capacity: _____ ÷ 1000 = _____ (L)

Ⓑ Volume: _____ = _____

Capacity: _____ = _____

Ⓒ Volume: _____ = _____

Capacity: _____ = _____

2. Which container has a capacity greater than 60 L
   but smaller than 80 L?   _____

3. Is the total capacity of **A** and **B** greater than
   the capacity of **C**?   _____

4. About how many times is the volume of **C** the
   volume of **B**?   _____

5. A box has the same volume as **B**. If the length and the width of the box
   are 35 cm and 33 cm respectively, what is the height?

   _____

6. 5 **B** are needed to hold all the water in an aquarium. What is the capacity
   of the aquarium? What is its volume?

   _____

7. Amy put a rock into **C**. Then it took 73.55 L of water to fill up **C**. What
   was the volume of the rock?

   _____

8. If **A** is filled with water to a depth of 38 cm, how many litres of water does
   it contain?

   _____

Capacity

comparing capacities of different objects

Write the total capacity of each group of juice in litres. Then answer the questions.

1.

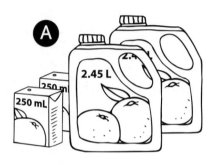

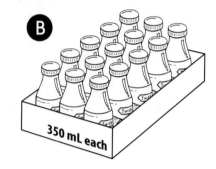

_____   _____   _____

2. Which group has the most juice?   _____

3. Mrs. Brown buys **B** and 5 more bottles of juice. How much juice does she buy in all?

_____

4. If Julie empties the juice in **C** into a cube with sides 18 cm each, will it overflow?

_____

5. How many **C** can fill a 1-m³ box?

_____

                    Quick Math Assessments | G.6

Unit Conversions

converting the units of mass

Fill in the blanks with "mg" or "t" to complete the diagram. Then write the appropriate unit to record the mass of each thing.

1.

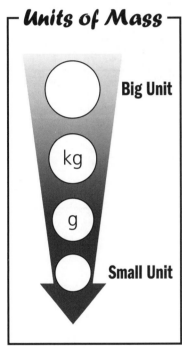

Units of Mass

Big Unit

kg

g

Small Unit

2.

3.

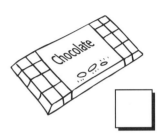

4.

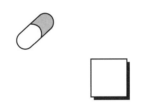

5.

Write each mass in two different ways.

6.   2980 g   _____ kg   _____ mg

7.   46.9 kg   _____ g   _____ t

8.   408 g   _____ kg   _____ mg

9.   53 kg   _____ g   _____ t

10.   26 000 g   _____ mg   _____ kg

Unit Conversions

Big unit $\xrightarrow{\text{x}}$ **Small** unit

e.g.   3.6 t = 3.6 x 1000 kg

= 36 000 kg

Small unit $\xrightarrow{\div}$ **Big** unit

e.g.   86 g = 86 ÷ 1000 kg

= 0.086 kg

Mass

finding and comparing masses

Answer the questions.

1. How many grams does each cookie weigh?

    _____

2. What is the weight of 20 cookies in grams? And in kilograms?

    _____

3. The total weight of a box of cookies and a cake is 2.2 kg. How heavy is the cake?

    _____

4. If Pam cuts the cake into 8 equal slices, how many kilograms does each slice weigh? How many grams?

    _____

Mass

solving problems related to masses of objects

Record each measure in two different units. Then answer the questions.

1.

326 g

_____ kg

_____ mg

2.

52 000 mg

_____ g

_____ kg

3.

Cookies
1.15 kg

_____ t

_____ g

4. A bag has 1000 onions. How heavy is the bag in kilograms?

_____

5. A box of apples weighs 3260 kg. How many apples are there in a box?

_____

6. There are 100 000 boxes of cookies in a carton. How many tonnes does a carton of cookies weigh?

_____

7. 5 children share a box of cookies equally. How many grams of cookies does each child get?

_____

8. A chef makes a dish with 10 onions. If there are 4 servings in a dish, how many kilograms of onions are there in each serving?

_____

Measurement

Skills	Level			
	1	2	3	4
estimate, measure, and record length, area, mass, capacity, and volume using metric measurement system				
estimate and measure quantities using metric units				
convert metric units				
convert square centimetres to square metres or vice versa				
construct rectangles, triangles, and parallelograms				
find the area relationships among rectangles, parallelograms, and triangles				
find areas of parallelograms and triangles using formulas				
find surface areas of rectangular and triangular prisms				
solve problems related to areas of triangular and rectangular prisms				
relate the height and the area of the base to the volume of a rectangular prism				
find the volume of a triangular prism by decomposing the volume of a rectangular prism				
solve problems related to volumes of triangular and rectangular prisms				
relate volume to capacity				
find appropriate units of masses				
solve problems related to mass and capacity				

Level 1 – Student shows little or no understanding of the concept and is rarely able to apply the required skills.

Level 2 – Student shows some understanding of the concept and is sometimes able to apply the required skills.

Level 3 – Student shows a good understanding of the concept and is usually able to apply the required skills.

Level 4 – Student shows an excellent understanding of the concept and is consistently able to apply the required skills.

Comments: _____

Geometry and Spatial Sense

Date:

Name:

Angles

measuring angles to 360°

Name each angle. Measure and record the size of it. Then answer the question.

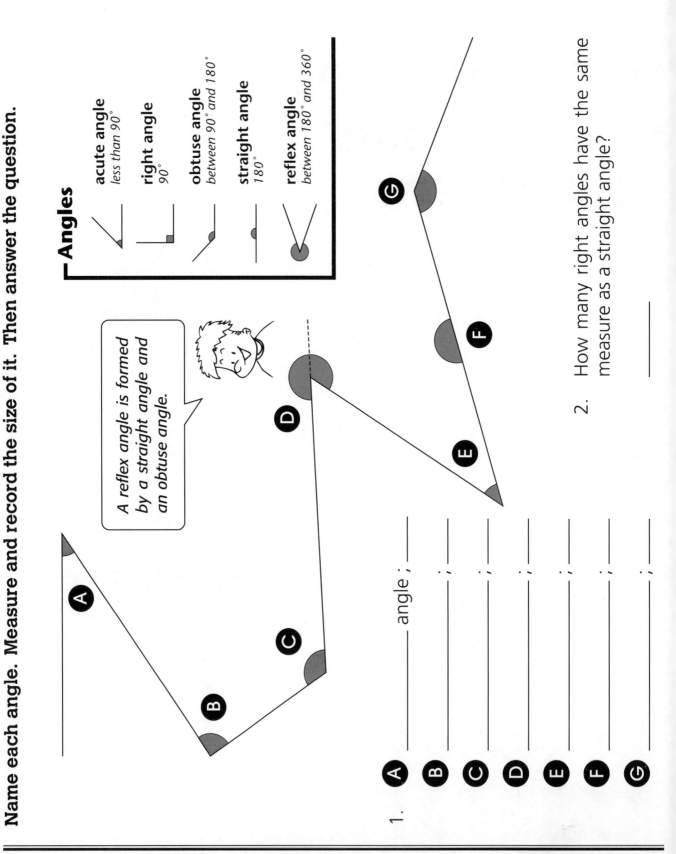

Angles

acute angle
less than 90°

right angle
90°

obtuse angle
between 90° and 180°

straight angle
180°

reflex angle
between 180° and 360°

A reflex angle is formed by a straight angle and an obtuse angle.

1. A _____ angle ; _____
    B _____ ; _____
    C _____ ; _____
    D _____ ; _____
    E _____ ; _____
    F _____ ; _____
    G _____ ; _____

2. How many right angles have the same measure as a straight angle?

    _____

Constructing Figures

constructing polygons with the given information

Follow the clues to contruct the figures. Measure and label the dimensions and angles. Then name the figures.

1. **quadrilateral ABCD**

   - AB = 5.5 cm
   - BC = AD = 3 cm
   - ∠BAD = ∠ABC = 110°

   _____
   name

2. **quadrilateral LMNO**

   - LO = 6 cm
   - ∠OLM = 75° and LM = 3 cm
   - ∠LMN = 105° and MN = 6 cm

   _____
   name

3. **polygon PQRST**

   - PQ = RS = 2.6 cm
   - QR = 3.5 cm
   - ∠QPT = 55°
   - ∠PQR = 205°
   - ∠QRS = 60°
   - connect S and T

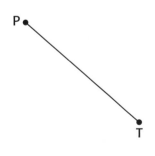

_____
name

Drawing 3-D Models

drawing top, front, and side views of 3-D models

Draw each model on the dot paper. Then draw the top, front, and side views of each model on the grid.

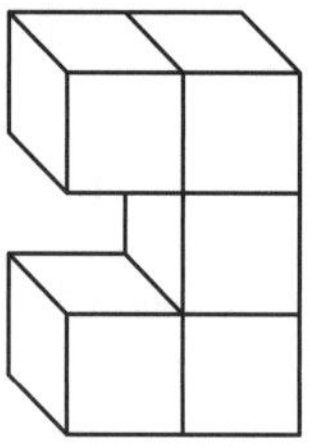

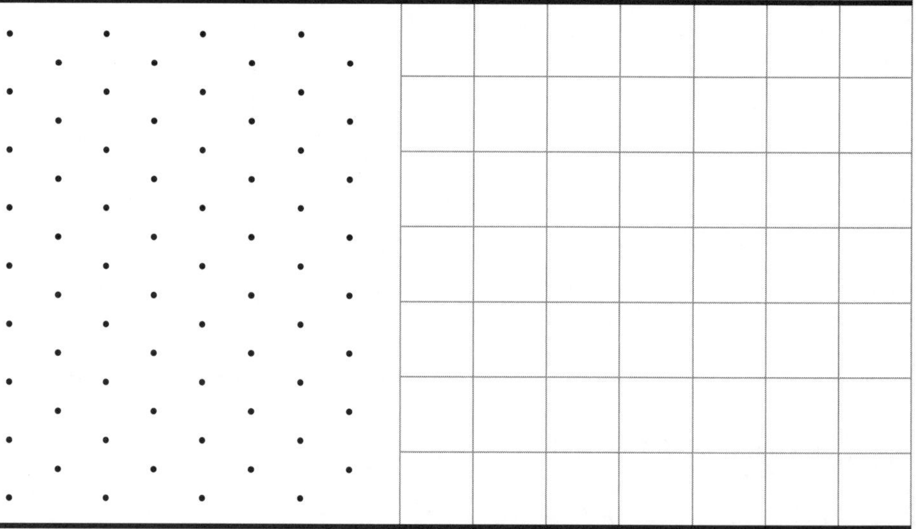

3.

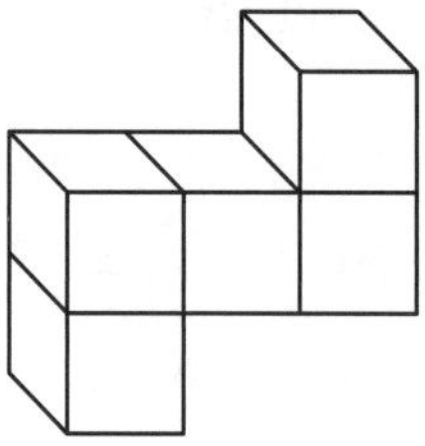

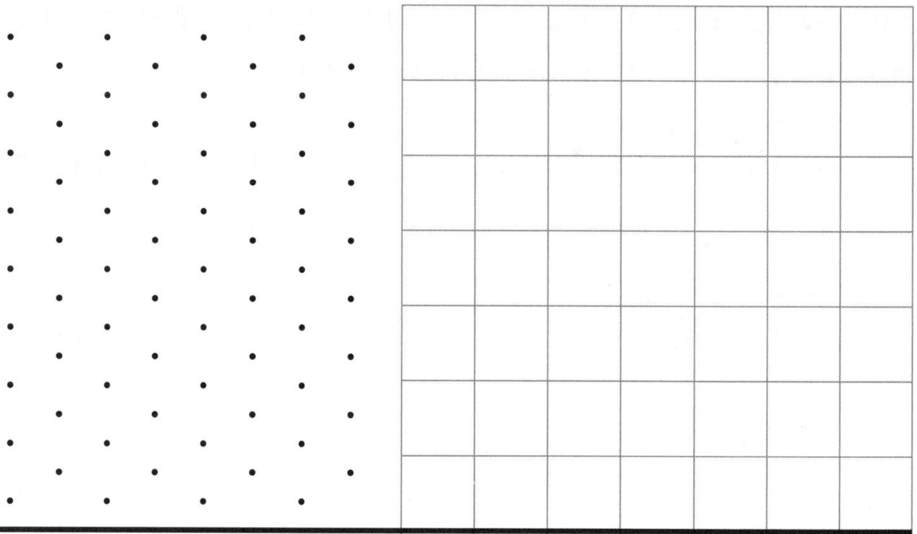

2.

1.

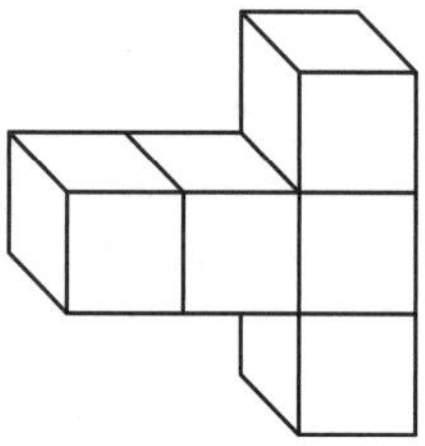

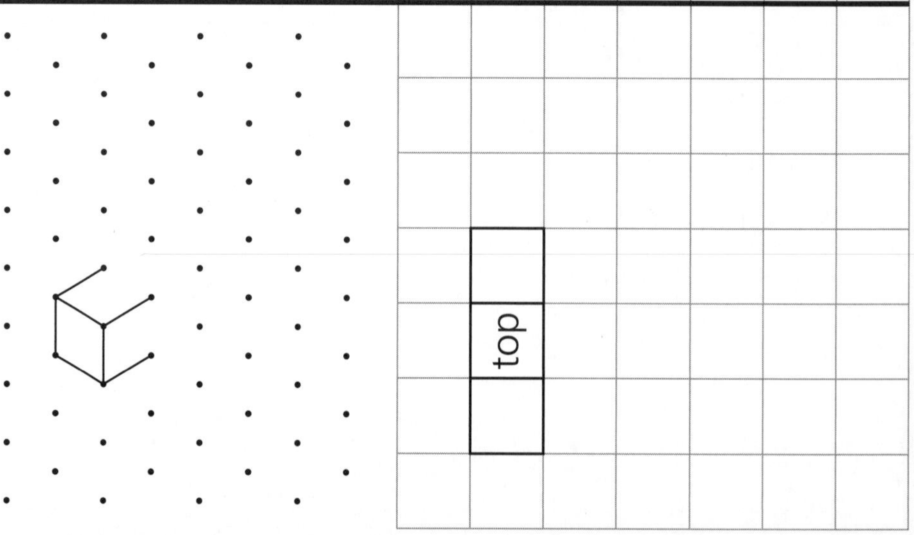

top

Combined Transformations

drawing images after combined transformations and writing the coordinates of images

Write the coordinates. Draw the images. Then describe the transformations.

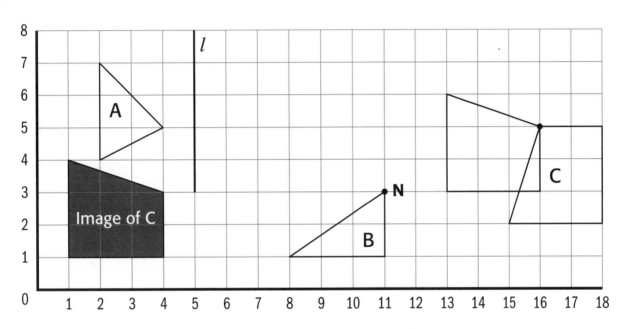

1. Write the coordinates of the vertices of each shape.

    A : _____   B : _____   C : _____

    _____   _____   _____

2. Draw the images of A and B.

    *   Reflect A in the line *l*. Then translate the image 6 squares right and 1 square up.

    *   Rotate B a $\frac{3}{4}$ turn counterclockwise about N. Then translate it 3 squares left and 2 squares down.

3. Describe a pair of transformations that moves C onto the image.

    _____

Congruent Figures

identifying and finding congruent figures

Measure and record the angles and sides of each triangle. Then fill in the blanks.

1. **Angle** ────────────

    ∠A = ____   ∠P = ____

    ∠B = ____   ∠Q = ____

    ∠C = ____   ∠R = ____

    Side ────────────

    AB = ____   PQ = ____

    BC = ____   QR = ____

    CA = ____   RP = ____

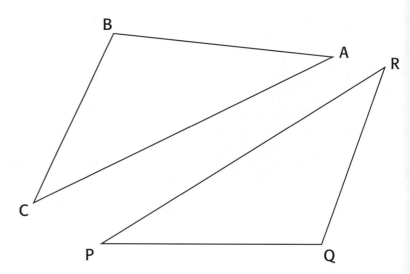

The corresponding angles and sides of these two triangles are the same, so they are _____ figures.

Measure and label the angles and sides of each triangle. Then colour the congruent triangles with the same colour.

2.

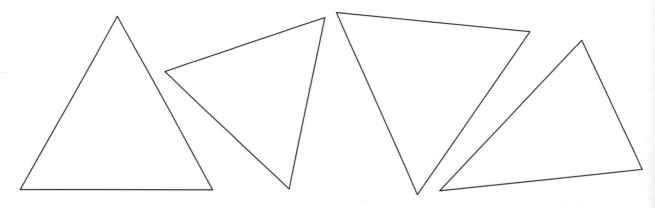

Similar Figures

identifying similar figures

Fill in the blanks to complete the sentences. Then colour the similar figures with the same colour.

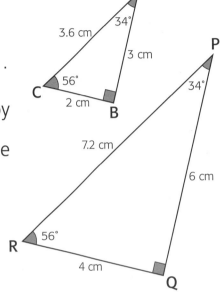

1. Any 2 figures are similar if

    - their corresponding angles are _____ .
      equal / not equal

    - each side length of one figure multiplied by
      the same number is _____ to the
      equal / not equal
      corresponding side length of the other figure.

    So, △ABC is _____ to △PQR.

2.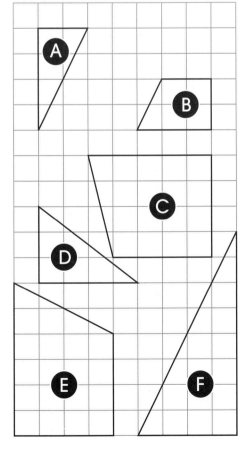

3.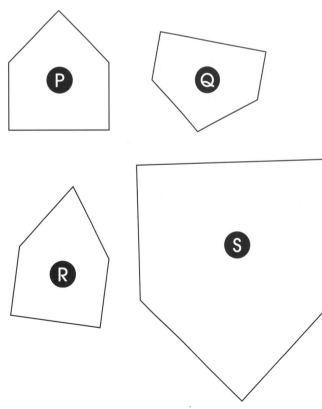

Rotational Symmetry

finding figures with rotational symmetry and their orders

Cut out the shapes. Then identify the shapes that have rotational symmetry and record the orders.

1.

	Has Rotational Symmetry Yes / No	Order
A		
B		
C		
D		

Order of Rotational Symmetry

Make a full turn of a figure. If it coincides with itself 4 times, it has a rotational symmetry of order 4.

e.g.   Make a full turn.

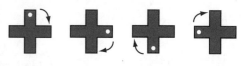

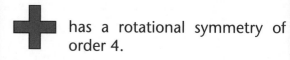 has a rotational symmetry of order 4.

Draw and label the figures.

2. P: a figure with rotational symmetry of order 4

   Q: a figure with rotational symmetry of order 2 and 2 lines of symmetry

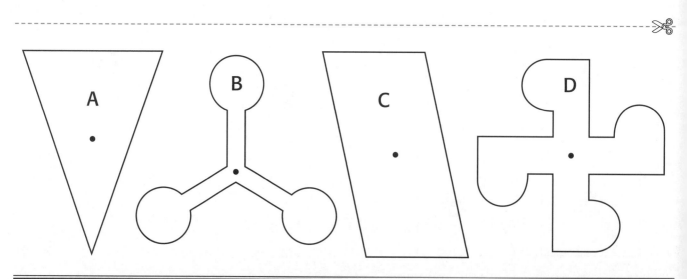

Tiling Patterns

describing and making tiling patterns by transformation

Read the description. Complete the tiling pattern.

1.

Translate the parallelogram to the right to complete the first row. Then reflect the whole row to form the second row and so on.

Use the given shapes to make tiling pattern. Then describe the pattern.

2.

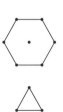

Description: _____

_____

Name: _____ Date: _____

Geometry and Spatial Sense

Skills	Level			
	1	2	3	4
sort and classify quadrilaterals by geometric properties related to symmetry, angles, and sides				
sort polygons according to the number of lines of symmetry and the order of rotational symmetry				
classify angles as acute, right, obtuse, or straight angles				
measure and construct angles using a protractor				
construct polygons with given angles and side measurements				
sketch and build 3-D models using connecting cubes with different views				
plot points and describe locations in a coordinate system				
perform combined transformations of a 2-D figure in a coordinate system				
create and analyse designs made by translation, reflection, or rotation of a shape				
identify congruent and similar figures				
make tiling patterns				

Level 1 – Student shows little or no understanding of the concept and is rarely able to apply the required skills.

Level 2 – Student shows some understanding of the concept and is sometimes able to apply the required skills.

Level 3 – Student shows a good understanding of the concept and is usually able to apply the required skills.

Level 4 – Student shows an excellent understanding of the concept and is consistently able to apply the required skills.

Comments: _____

 Quick Math Assessments | G.6

Patterning and Algebra

Equations

writing simple equations using variables and solving equations

Check the equation that matches each situation. Then find the answer.

1. Joe and Sabrina have 15 marbles in all. Sabrina has 6 marbles. How many marbles does Joe have?

   A ☐ 🌀 + 6 = 15

   B ☐ 15 + 🌀 = 6

Reverse + **and** −
x **and** ÷

e.g. ▲ x 5 = 75 ← "x" problem

Think: 75 ÷ 5 ← reverse operation "÷"
= __15__

So, 15 x 5 = __75__

▲ is 15.

Joe has _____ marbles.

2. Mrs. Cowan pays $20 for a cake and her change is $5. How much is the cake?

   A ☐ y + 20 = 5

   B ☐ 20 − y = 5

   The cake is $ _____ .

Write an equation for each problem. Then solve it.

3. 3 boxes of chocolates cost $12. What is the cost of a box?

   _____ = the cost of a box
   a letter

   3 _____ = _____

4. A group of children share 16 candies. Each child gets 2 candies. How many children are there?

_____

_____

Number Patterns
finding pattern rules and extending patterns

Find the difference between every 2 numbers. Then write the pattern rule and find the 9th term of each pattern.

1. a.

    b. Each number added _____ the previous number added.
        _{doubles / triples}

        So, "_____" is part of the pattern rule.
        _{x 2 / x 3}

    c. Pattern rule: Start at _____ . _____

        _____

        | The 9th term: |

2. a.

    b. Each number taken away is _____ of the previous number
        _{one third / one half}
        taken away.

        So, "_____" is part of the pattern rule.
        _{÷ 2 / ÷ 3}

    c. Pattern rule: Start at _____ . _____

        _____

        | The 9th term: |

Number Patterns

matching the number patterns with the pattern rules, finding the next two terms, and writing pattern rules for Input/Output machines

Match the pattern rules with the number patterns. Write the letters. Then find the next 2 terms.

1. ☐ 6, 18, 42, 90, _____ , _____

2. ☐ 5, 9, 21, 57, _____ , _____

3. ☐ 2, 5, 11, 23, _____ , _____

4. ☐ 52, 98, 190, 374, _____ , _____

5. ☐ 128, 192, 288, 432, _____ , _____

A × 2, + 1

B + 3, × 2

C − 2, × 3

D − 3, × 2

E ÷ 2, × 3

Find the outputs. Write the pattern rules for the input and the output. Then find the 10th input and output.

6. ×2 +3

Input	Output
5	
7	
9	
11	

Pattern rule

• input: _____

• output: _____

The 10th: _____ _____
           input   output

7. −4 ×3

Input	Output
12	
13	
14	
15	

Pattern rule

• input: _____

• output: _____

The 10th: _____ _____
           input   output

 Quick Math Assessments | G.6

Solve Problems Using Patterns

solving problems using patterns

Follow the patterns to find the correct number of marbles in the boxes. Write the pattern rules. Then answer the questions.

1. Joe puts 8 marbles in box 1; 13 in box 2; 23 in box 3; and 43 in box 4.

Box	No. of Marbles
1	8
2	13
3	23
4	43
5	
6	
7	

2. Pattern rule:

_____

_____

3. How many marbles are there in box 9?

_____

4. Sue has 386 marbles in box 1; 194 in box 2; 98 in box 3; and 50 in box 4.

Box	No. of Marbles
1	
2	
3	
4	
5	
6	
7	

5. Pattern rule:

_____

_____

6. Which box contains 5 marbles?

_____

Number Patterns

using Input/Output machines to find ordered pairs and plotting them on graphs

Complete the Input/Output machines. Then graph the data and answer the questions.

1.

x3 — -2

Input	Output	Ordered Pair (Input,Output)
2	4	(2,4)
4		
6		
8		
10		

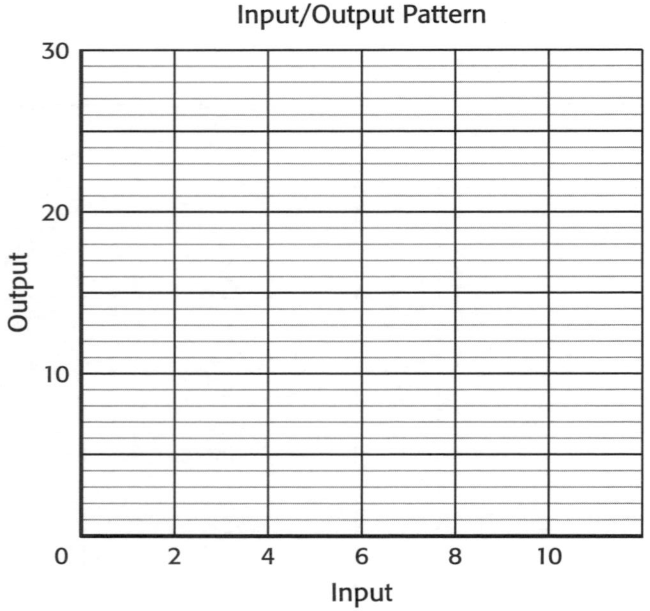

Input/Output Pattern

Output

30

20

10

0   2   4   6   8   10
Input

If the input number is 3, the output number is _____.

2.

÷2 — +1

Input	Output	Ordered Pair (Input,Output)
10		
20		
30		
40		
50		

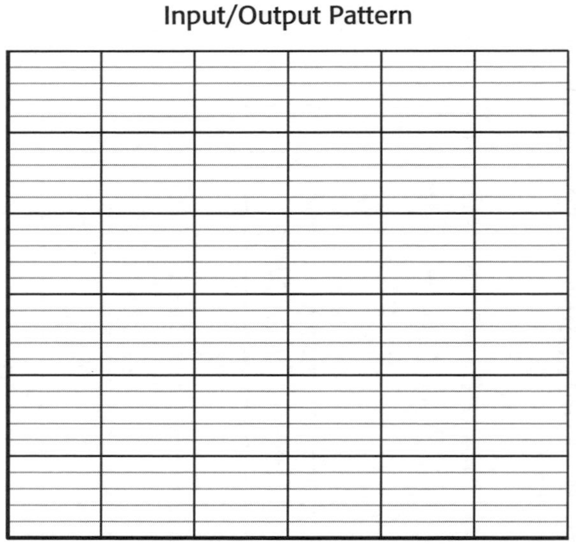

Input/Output Pattern

If the output number is 29, the input number is _____.

Geometric Patterns

identifying geometric patterns

Draw the next figure for each pattern. Then write a pattern rule to describe how the number of shapes changes.

1.

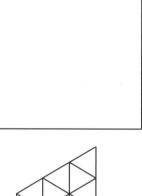

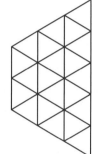

Number of Small Triangles

Pattern Rule: _____

2.

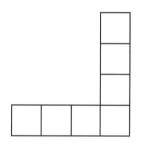

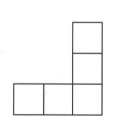

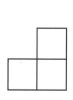

Number of Small Squares

Pattern Rule: _____

Geometric Patterns

finding patterns in geometry

Look at the growing pattern made with centimetre sticks. Follow the pattern to draw the next frame. Complete the table. Then answer the questions.

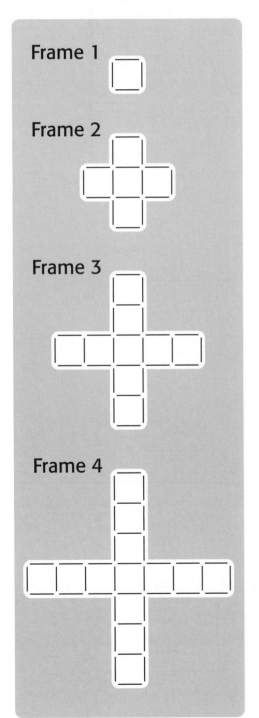

Frame 1

Frame 2

Frame 3

Frame 4

1. Frame 5 ━━━━━━━━━━━━━━━━━━━━━━

2.

Frame	No. of ☐	No. of / Used	Perimeter (cm)
1	*1*	*4*	*4*
2			
3			
4			
5			

3. How is the perimeter related to the number of squares?

_____

_____

4. How is the number of sticks used related to the number of squares?

_____

_____

5. Predict the number of sticks used and the perimeter of Frame 8.

_____

6. Write the frame number and the perimeter of each frame as an ordered pair. Then make a line graph to show the data.

Ordered Pair
(Frame no.,Perimeter)

_____

(1,4)

_____

_____

_____

_____

Perimeter of Each Frame

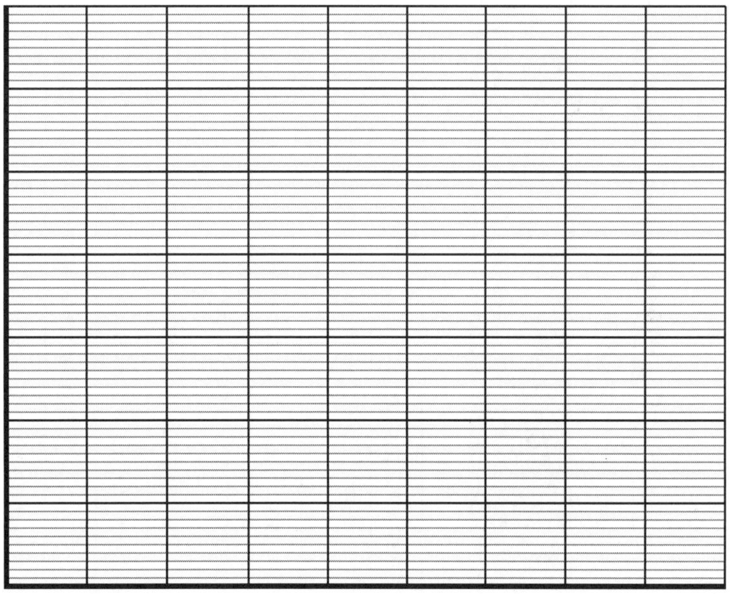

7. Use the graph above to find

a. the perimeter of Frame 8.   _____

b. the frame that has a perimeter of 68 cm.   _____

Patterning and Algebra

Skills	Level			
	1	2	3	4
make tables of values for growing and shrinking patterns and describe the pattern rules				
list the ordered pairs of a pattern and plot them in a graph				
find the term number of a given term in a pattern that is represented by a pattern rule in words, a table of values, or a graph				
solve equations, graphs, and relate Input/Output machines				
identify geometric patterns and represent them numerically				
extend and create repeating patterns that result from rotations				
identify quantities in an equation that vary and those remain constant				
use variables for unknowns in simple algebraic expressions and equations to describe relationships				
find the solution to a simple equation with one variable				
solve problems involving 2 or 3 variables				

Level 1 – Student shows little or no understanding of the concept and is rarely able to apply the required skills.
Level 2 – Student shows some understanding of the concept and is sometimes able to apply the required skills.
Level 3 – Student shows a good understanding of the concept and is usually able to apply the required skills.
Level 4 – Student shows an excellent understanding of the concept and is consistently able to apply the required skills.

Comments:

Data Management and Probability

Mean, Median, Mode

finding mean, median, and mode of a set of data

Look at the grid. Record the heights of the nine objects in metres from shortest to tallest. Then answer the questions.

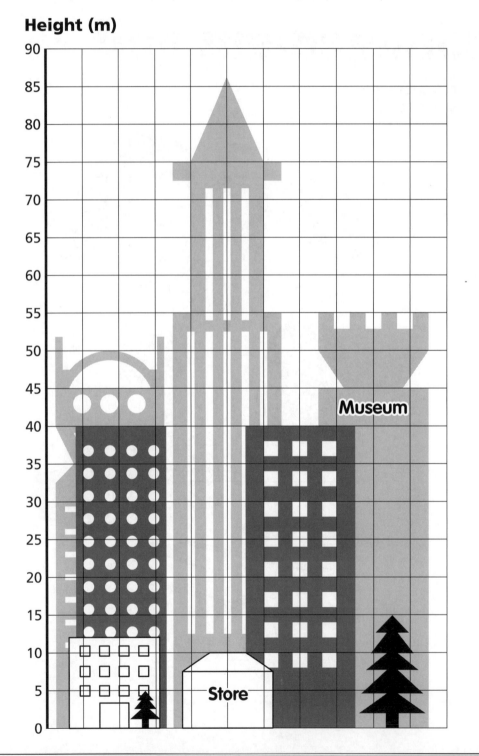

Height (m)

1. In order:

   shortest

   ⎯⎯⎯⎯⎯

   ⎯⎯⎯⎯⎯

   ⎯⎯⎯⎯⎯

   ⎯⎯⎯⎯⎯

   ⎯⎯⎯⎯⎯

   ⎯⎯⎯⎯⎯

   ⎯⎯⎯⎯⎯

   ⎯⎯⎯⎯⎯

   tallest

2. Find the mean, median, and mode of the heights of the objects.

Mean = _____ ÷ _____

     = _____

Median = _____

Mode = _____

Mean	= total ÷ no. of addends
Median	= the middle number when data are put in order
Mode	= the number that occurs most often

3. If a tower which is taller than the museum is included in this set of data, do you think the new mean of the objects will be greater or less than the old one? Explain.

_____

_____

4. If a 15-m tall building is included in this set of data, what will the new mean, median, and mode be?

Mean: _____

Median: _____

Mode: _____

5. If there were no museum in this set of data, what would be the new mean, median, and mode of the heights of the objects?

Mean: _____

Median: _____

Mode: _____

Circle Graph

reading circle graphs to solve problems

Measure the angles to complete the table. Then answer the questions.

1.

Colour	Angle of Measure	Fraction
Yellow		
Green		
Blue		
Others		

Children's Favourite Colours

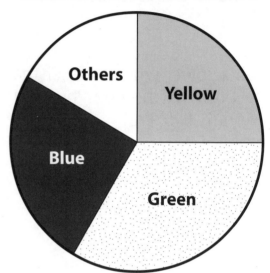

2.   Which is the most popular colour?   _____

3.   What fraction of the children like yellow or blue?   _____

4.   Give an example of colour that can be included in
     the "Others" section.   _____

5.   If 60 children are surveyed, how many children like
     green? (Think: What number is one third of 60?)   _____

6.   If 100 children are surveyed, how many children
     like blue?   _____

Coordinates

locating and plotting points on a coordinate grid

Ordered Pairs

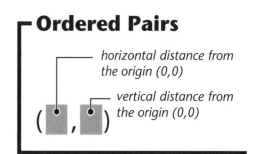

horizontal distance from the origin (0,0)

vertical distance from the origin (0,0)

(▪ , ▪)

Locate and plot the points on the grid. Then answer the questions.

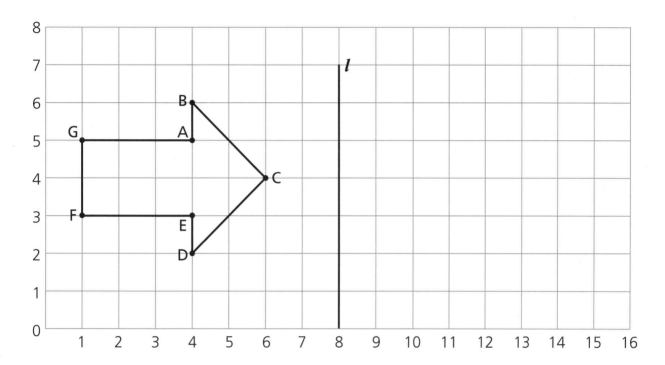

1. Coordinates

    A (____ , ____)

    B _____

    C _____

    D _____

    E _____

    F _____

    G _____

2. Reflect the arrow over the line l. Draw the image on the grid. Then label the vertices from P to V and write their coordinates.

    _____

    _____

3. Move the image of the arrow 1 unit up and 2 units left. Rotate a $\frac{1}{4}$ turn clockwise about (8,5). Name it Y. Then circle the vertices of Y located on the horizontal line if there are any.

Scatter Plot
interpreting data from scatter plots

Look at each scatter plot. Check the answers. Then answer the questions.

1. The 2 quantities that each point on the plot represents:

    Prices and Items Sold

    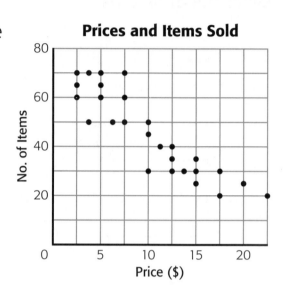

    | A | the price of an item

    | B | the temperature

    | C | the number of items in a box

    | D | the number of items sold

2. Does the plot show any trend? If yes, describe the trend.

    | A | Yes. It shows _____ trend. _____

    an upward / a downward

    _____

    | B | No, it does not.

3. **Time Spent on Studying and Math Scores**

    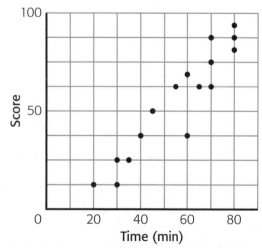

    Is there a trend in the graph? Explain.

    _____

    _____

    _____

    _____

Probability

describing probabilities using decimals, fractions, and percents

Use a decimal, a fraction, and a percent to describe the probability of each event.

1. Draw a card without looking. Find the probability of drawing

    a. a card with a letter "A":

    _____

    b. a card with a lower case letter:

    _____

    c. a card with a number:

    _____

A	A	M	D
L	g	d	E
J	H	e	j
b	y	m	F
A	B	G	h

2. Draw a ball without looking. Record the colour of the ball drawn and put the ball back into the bag. Do this 100 times. Find the probability of drawing

    a. a red ball: _____

    b. a yellow ball: _____

    c. a blue ball: _____

    d. a coloured ball: _____

    red: 10
    blue: 25
    yellow: 15

    50 balls

Experimental and Theoretical Probabilities

finding experimental and theoretical probabilities of different events

Find the theoretical probabilities of rolling a die numbered from 1 to 6. Then look at the records of the children. Solve the problems.

—— Experimental Probabilities —— | —— Theoretical Probabilities —

$$\text{Experimental Probability} = \frac{\text{No. of Times an Outcome Occurs}}{\text{No. of Times the Experiment is Conducted}}$$

$$\text{Theoretical Probability} = \frac{\text{No. of Favourable Outcomes}}{\text{No. of Possible Outcomes}}$$

1. The theoretical probabilities of getting each number:

    1: _____   2: _____   3: _____

    4: _____   5: _____   6: _____

2. Tom and Sandra rolled the die 30 times. Help each child find the experimental probability of getting each number.

    a. Tom's Record

    1: _____   2: _____   3: _____

    4: _____   5: _____   6: _____

    b. Sandra's Record

    1: _____   2: _____   3: _____

    4: _____   5: _____   6: _____

	Tom's Record (no. of times)	Sandra's Record (no. of times)
1	4	2
2	5	7
3	5	6
4	4	3
5	6	2
6	6	10

Tree Diagram

finding probabilities using a tree diagram

Complete the tree diagram to show the choices of a couch. Then answer the questions.

1.

Colour	Material	Style	Combination
(black / brown / white)	(fabric / leather)	(3-seat / 2-seat)	

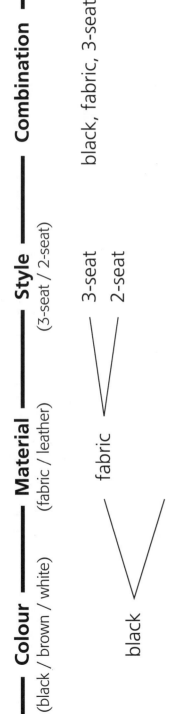

black — fabric — 3-seat — black, fabric, 3-seat

2-seat

2. What is the probability that a customer will choose

a. a black leather 3-seat couch? _____   b. a 2-seat couch? _____

c. a fabric 2-seat couch? _____   d. a white couch? _____

Data Management and Probability

Skills	Level			
	1	2	3	4
collect data by conducting a survey or an experiment				
select an appropriate group of population to collect data				
collect and organize data and display them in charts, tables, and graphs with appropriate titles, labels, and scales				
use scatter plots to represent data and describe the trends shown				
interpret data and tell the relationships between two sets of data				
find the means and medians of different sets of data and do comparison				
use tree diagrams to find probability				
find theoretical probabilities and write them as ratios				
predict the frequency of an outcome of a simple probability experiment or game				
relate probability and percent				

Level 1 – Student shows little or no understanding of the concept and is rarely able to apply the required skills.

Level 2 – Student shows some understanding of the concept and is sometimes able to apply the required skills.

Level 3 – Student shows a good understanding of the concept and is usually able to apply the required skills.

Level 4 – Student shows an excellent understanding of the concept and is consistently able to apply the required skills.

Comments: _____

Answers

p.6 Large Numbers

1.

Millions			Thousands			Units		
H	T	O	H	T	O	H	T	O
	3	1	2	4	6	5	3	9
			4	5	0	0	0	0
		1	4	7	5	0	0	0

2. 31 246 539, 14 750 000, 4 500 000
3. A: Thirty-one million two hundred forty-six thousand five hundred thirty-nine ;
   30 000 000 + 1 000 000 + 200 000 + 40 000 + 6000 + 500 + 30 + 9
   B: Four million five hundred thousand ;
   4 000 000 + 500 000
   C: Fourteen million seven hundred fifty thousand ;
   10 000 000 + 4 000 000 + 700 000 + 50 000
4. 37 000 000 ; 36 500 000 ; 36 540 000
5. 11 000 000 ; 10 700 000 ; 10 650 000

p.7 Common Multiple

1. Star: 4, 6, 8, 10, 12, 14, 16, 18, 20, 22, 24, 26, 28, 30
   Circle: 6, 9, 12, 15, 18, 21, 24, 27, 30
2. 6, 12, 18, 24, 30   3. 6
4. 4 ; 8 ; 12 ; 16 ; 20 ; 24
   6 ; 12 ; 18 ; 24 ; 30 ; 36
   common multiples: 12, 24 ; L.C.M.: 12
5. 5 ; 10 ; 15 ; 20 ; 25 ; 30
   10 ; 20 ; 30 ; 40 ; 50 ; 60
   common multiples: 10, 20, 30 ; L.C.M.: 10

p.8 Prime and Composite Numbers

1. 2 ; 2
2. 1, 2, 3, 6, 7, 14, 21, 42 ; composite
3. 1, 2, 4, 5, 10, 20 ; composite
4. 1, 19 ; prime   5. 1, 3, 9 ; composite
6. 17, 19   7. (Individual answer)
8. 2

p.9 Integers

1.
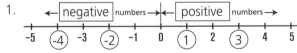

2. Negative ; left   3. Positive ; right
4. +2 kg   5. +$15
6. -30°C   7. -4 points
(Individual answers for questions 8 to 10)

p.10 Order of Operations

1. 34 – (12 ÷ 3); 34 – 4 ; 30
2. 9 + (5 x 2); 9 + 10 ; 19
3. (2 + 3) x 6 ; 5 x 6 ; 30
4. 18 + (6 ÷ 2); 18 + 3 ; 21
5. (5 x 6) ÷ 3 ; 30 ÷ 3 ; 10   6. 9 x (8 – 3); 9 x 5 ; 45
7. 52 + (6 x 7); 94   8. 26 – (14 ÷ 2); 19
9. (36 + 3) ÷ 3 = 13   10. 7 x (2 + 1) = 21

p.11 Addition and Subtraction

1.
```
  ②①
  224 ;   200
  475     500
  392     400
+ 718 + 700
 1809    1800
```
2.
```
  ①①
  321 ;   300
  219     200
  356     400
+ 142 + 100
 1038    1000
```
3. 5858 ;
```
  5858
+ 7966
 13824
```
4. 31563 ;
```
  31563
+ 13645
  45208
```
5. 45803 ;
```
  45803
+ 18726
  64529
```
6. 23191 ;
```
  23191
+ 15371
  38562
```
7. 57970 ;
```
  57970
+ 36288
  94258
```

p.12 Multiplication

1.
```
   221
 x  67
  1547
 13260
 14807
```
2.
```
   472
 x  29
  4248
  9440
 13688
```
3.
```
   762
 x  58
  6096
 38100
 44196
```
4.
```
   358
 x  61
   358
 21480
 21838
```
5.
```
   844
 x  35
  4220
 25320
 29540
```
6. 4080 batteries ;
```
   255
 x  16
  1530
  2550
  4080
```

7. unreasonable   8. reasonable   9. reasonable

p.13 Division

1.
```
      232 R 5 ; 232 x 12 = 2784 ;
  12)2789       2784 + 5 = 2789
     24
     38
     36
     29
     24
      5
```
2. A:
```
        190 R 15 ; 190 x 38 = 7220 ;
   38)7235         7220 + 15 = 7235
      38
     343
     342
      15
```
   B:
```
        422 R 14 ; 422 x 19 = 8018 ;
   19)8032         8018 + 14 = 8032
      76
      43
      38
      52
      38
      14
```

Answers

C:
```
      405 R8
15) 6083
    60
    ───
    83
    75
    ──
     8
```
405 x 15 = 6075 ;
6075 + 8 = 6083

D:
```
       17 R89
92) 1653
    92
    ───
    733
    644
    ───
     89
```
17 x 92 = 1564 ;
1564 + 89 = 1653

p.14 Decimals

1. 1.283 ; 1 + 0.2 + 0.08 + 0.003 ; one and two hundred eighty-three thousandths
2. 2.065 ; 2 + 0.06 + 0.005
3. 15.608 ; fifteen and six hundred eight thousandths
4. 403.079 ; four hundred three and seventy-nine thousandths
5. 3 + 0.2 + 0.05 + 0.004 ; three and two hundred fifty-four thousandths

p.15 Decimals

1. 24.12 ;
   24.16 ;
   least to greatest: 24.122, 24.156, 24.187
   24.122   24.156   *24.187*
   24.1   24.15   24.2
2. 36.32 ;
   36.38 ;
   36.35 ;
   greatest to least: 36.381, 36.345, 36.318
   36.318   36.345   36.381
   36.3   36.4
3. 3.465, 3.654, 4.365, 4.635 ; 4.636
4. 2.008, 2.081, 8.012, 12.008 ; 12.009

p.16 Adding and Subtracting Decimals

1.
```
   ①①
   2 . 6 8 9
 + 1 . 2 4 8
 ───────────
 [3].[9][3][7]
```

2.
```
    ①①①
    4 . 3 7 9
 +  5 . 8 9 3
 ────────────
 [1][0][2][7][2]
```

3. 5.684
4. 9.523 ; 2.977
5.
```
   7 . 5 0 0  ;   7 . 5 0 0
 + 3 . 2 7 7    − 3 . 2 7 7
 ──────────    ──────────
 1 0 . 7 7 7     4 . 2 2 3
```
6a. 2.5 + 0.375 = 2.875 ; There is 2.875 L of juice in all.
 b. 2.5 − 0.375 = 2.125 ; There is 2.125 L more.
7. 2.885 − 1.57 = 1.315 ; The other one is 1.315 m long.

p.17 Multiplying Decimals

1. 58.058
2. 113.877
3. 70.112
4. 47.535
5. 427
6. 20.314 x 10 ; 203.14
7. 1.74 x 10 000 ; 17 400
8. 0.07 x 1000 ; 70
9. 0.2061
10. 125.3 x 0.001 ; 0.1253
11. 1.5 x 0.1 ; 0.15
12. 0.18 x 0.001; 0.00018

p.18 Dividing Decimals

1.
```
    0.6 8 1
 4) 2.7 2 4
    2 4
    ───
    3 2
    3 2
    ───
      4
      4
```
2. A: 1.992
```
    1.9 9 2
 3) 5.9 7 6
    3
    ───
    2 9
    2 7
    ───
    2 7
    2 7
    ───
      6
      6
```
B: 1.068
```
    1.0 6 8
 7) 7.4 7 6
    7
    ───
    4 7
    4 2
    ───
    5 6
    5 6
```

C: 1.117
```
    1.1 1 7
 8) 8.9 3 6
    8
    ───
    9
    8
    ───
    1 3
     8
    ───
    5 6
    5 6
```
D: 2.044
```
    2.0 4 4
 6) 1 2.2 6 4
    1 2
    ────
    2 6
    2 4
    ───
    2 4
    2 4
```

3. 1258.4
4. 20.94 ÷ 0.01 ; 2094
5. 3.654 ÷ 0.1 ; 36.54
6. 28.204 ÷ 0.001 ; 28 204

p.19 Fractions

(Suggested answers for the first two equivalent fractions)

1. $\frac{36}{40}$; $\frac{9}{10}$; $\frac{9}{10}$
2. $\frac{20}{30}$; $\frac{2}{3}$; $\frac{2}{3}$
3. $\frac{96}{100}$; $\frac{24}{25}$; $\frac{24}{25}$
4. $\frac{24}{36}$; $\frac{6}{9}$; $\frac{2}{3}$
5. $\frac{32}{48}$; $\frac{8}{12}$; $\frac{2}{3}$
6. $\frac{48}{60}$; $\frac{12}{15}$; $\frac{4}{5}$
7. $\frac{4}{5}$, $\frac{17}{20}$, $\frac{9}{10}$
8. $\frac{3}{20}$, $\frac{1}{4}$, $\frac{2}{5}$
9. $\frac{1}{3}$, $\frac{4}{7}$, $\frac{16}{21}$
10. $\frac{11}{18}$, $\frac{2}{3}$, $\frac{5}{6}$

p.20 Adding and Subtracting Fractions

1. 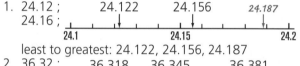 ; 9 ; 3
2. ; 6 ; 2
3. $\frac{4}{16}$; $\frac{1}{4}$
4. $\frac{5}{10}$; $\frac{1}{2}$
5. $\frac{12}{12}$; 1
6. $\frac{2}{8}$; $\frac{1}{4}$
7. $\frac{10}{15}$; $\frac{2}{3}$
8. $\frac{4}{6}$; $\frac{2}{3}$
9. $\frac{3}{9}$; $\frac{1}{3}$
10. $\frac{8}{10}$; $\frac{4}{5}$

p.21 Percent

1. 0.45 ; 45%
2. $\frac{82}{100}$; 0.82
3. 54% ; $\frac{54}{100}$
4. 0.09 ; 9%
5. $\frac{36}{100}$; 0.36
6. 70% ; $\frac{70}{100}$
Way 1: 20 ; 2 ; 10 ; 10
Way 2: 20 ; 10 ; 5 ; 5 ; 10 ; 10
7. 15
8. 1
9. 16

p.22 Ratio

1a. 3:5   b. 5:8   c. 3:8
2a. 12:4   b. 12:16   c. 16:4
3a. 28:10   b. 28:16   c. 6:16   d. 16:48

p.23 Rate

1. $2.24/box   2. 12 sausages/plate
3. 4 assignments/day   4. 9 stickers/child
5. 78 words/minute
6a. 36 ; 54 ; 30 ; 45
 b. Susan

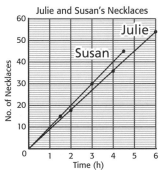

Julie and Susan's Necklaces

p.26 Time, Distance, and Average Speed

1. 452 ; 2 ; 226   2. 564 ; 3 ; 188
3. 326 ; 2 ; 163   4. 260 ; 4 ; 65
5. the plane
6a. 226 ; 452 ; 678 ; 904 ; 1130   b. 1356 km

p.27 Area of a Parallelogram

1. Trace the dotted line labelled 11 cm. ; 20 ; 11 ; 220
2. Trace the dotted line labelled 14 m. ; 9 x 14 ; 126 (m²)
3. A: Trace the dotted line labelled 17 m. ;
     22 x 17 ; 374 (m²)
   B: Trace the dotted line labelled 19 cm. ;
     8 x 19 ; 152 (cm²)
   C: Trace the dotted line labelled 32 cm. ;
     40 x 32 ; 1280 (cm²)

p.28 Area of a Triangle

1. base ; height
2. A: 4 ; 4.5 ; 9   B: 5 x 7.2 ÷ 2 ; 18
   C: 6.4 x 5 ÷ 2 ; 16   D: 6 x 4.8 ÷ 2 ; 14.4

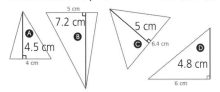

p.29 Surface Area of a Rectangular Prism

1. 2 green rectangles: 10 ; 8 ; 160
   2 red rectangles: 10 x 1.5 x 2 ; 30
   2 yellow rectangles: 8 x 1.5 x 2 ; 24
   160 ; 30 ; 24 ; 214
2. 6 x 8 x 2 = 96 ; 15 x 8 x 2 = 240 ; 15 x 6 x 2 = 180
   Surface area: 96 + 240 + 180 = 516 (cm²)

3. 12 x 6 x 2 = 144 ; 12 x 10 x 2 = 240 ; 6 x 10 x 2 = 120
   Surface area: 144 + 240 + 120 = 504 (cm²)

p.30 Surface Area of a Rectangular Prism

1. 1112 ; B   2. 408 cm² ; C   3. 734 cm² ; A
4. Surface area: 12 x 14 x 2 + 12 x 25 x 2 + 14 x 25 x 2 =
   1636 (cm²) ; 1636 cm² of wrapping paper is needed.
5. Surface area: 12 x 28 x 2 + 12 x 25 x 2 + 28 x 25 x 2
   = 2672 (cm²) ;
   She needs 2672 cm² of wrapping paper.

p.31 Surface Area of a Triangular Prism

1. 6 ; 8 ; 24 x 2 ; 48
   15 ; 10 ; 15 ; 6 ; 15 ; 8 ; 150 + 90 + 120 ; 360
   48 ; 360 ; 408
2. Area of triangular faces: 9 x 12 ÷ 2 x 2 = 108 (cm²)
   Area of rectangular faces: 10 x 15 + 10 x 9 + 10 x 12
   = 360 (cm²)
   Surface area: 108 + 360 = 468 (cm²)
3. Area of triangular faces: 3 x 4 ÷ 2 x 2 = 12 (cm²)
   Area of rectangular faces: 9 x 5 + 9 x 4 + 9 x 3 =
   108 (cm²)
   Surface area: 12 + 108 = 120 (cm²)

p.32-33 Surface Area and Volume

1. A: Surface area: 12 x 10 x 2 + 18 x 10 x 2 + 12 x 18 x 2
      = 1032 (cm²)
      Volume: 12 x 10 x 18 = 2160 (cm³)
   B: Surface area: 13 x 10 x 2 + 13 x 9 x 2 + 10 x 9 x 2
      = 674 (cm²)
      Volume: 13 x 10 x 9 = 1170 (cm³)
   C: Surface area: 25 x 7 x 2 + 25 x 10 x 2 + 7 x 10 x 2
      = 990 (cm²)
      Volume: 25 x 7 x 10 = 1750 (cm³)
   D: Surface area: 6 x 4 x 2 + 6 x 21 x 2 + 4 x 21 x 2 =
      468 (cm²)
      Volume: 6 x 4 x 21 = 504 (cm³)
   E: Surface area: 18 x 4 x 2 + 18 x 21 x 2 + 4 x 21 x 2
      = 1068 (cm²)
      Volume: 21 x 18 x 4 = 1512 (cm³)
2. E   3. A   4. No
5. The surface area is 768 cm² and the volume is 1008 cm³.

p.34 Volume of a Triangular Prism

1. (10 x 12 x 9.5) ÷ 2 = 570 (cm³)
2. (4 x 6 x 8.8) ÷ 2 = 105.6 (m³)
3. (2 x 2 x 1.2) ÷ 2 = 2.4 (dm³)
4. (13.8 x 6 x 4) ÷ 2 = 165.6 (cm³)
5. (6 x 8.6 x 5) ÷ 2 = 129 (m³)

p.35 Volume of a Rectangular Prism

1. A: 5 cm   B: 13 cm
   C: 7.2 cm   D: 10.6 cm
2. Volume of the small prism: 5 x 4 x 5 = 100 (cm³)
   Volume of the solid: 640 – 100 = 540 (cm³)
   The volume of the solid is 540 cm³.
3. Volume of E: 7.2 x 3 x 7 = 151.2 (cm³)
   Volume of "T": 302.4 + 151.2 = 453.6 (cm³)
   The volume of letter "T" is 453.6 cm³.

Answers

p.36 Unit Conversions

1. 5400 ; 5.4
2. 46 500 ; 46.5
3. 390 ; 0.39
4. 86 ; 0.086
5. 68 ; 68 000 000
6. 495 ; 0.495
7. 0.875 ; 875 000
8. 540 ; 540 000

p.37 Volume and Capacity

1. 3 x 1.5 x 2 = 9 (m³) = 9000 (L)
   It can hold 9000 L of water.
2. 450 000 cm³ = 450 L;
   9000 – 450 = 8550 (L)
   It can hold 8550 L of water now.
3. Capacity of the box:
   8 x 10 x 5 = 400 (cm³) = 0.4 (L)
   (9000 ÷ 2) ÷ 0.4 = 4500 ÷ 0.4 = 11 250
   Jason needs to empty the box 11 250 times.
4. 6 x 3 x 4 = 72 (m³) = 72 000 L
   The new water tank can hold 72 000 L of water.

p.38-39 Volume and Capacity of a Rectangular Prism

1. A: Volume: 42 ; 30 ; 63 ; 79 380
   Capacity: 79 380 ; 79.38
   B: Volume: 22 x 14 x 75 ; 23 100 (cm³)
   Capacity: 23 100 ÷ 1000 ; 23.1 (L)
   C: Volume: 68 x 34 x 40 ; 92 480 (cm³)
   Capacity: 92 480 ÷ 1000 ; 92.48 (L)
2. A   3. Yes   4. about 4 times
5. Height: 23 100 ÷ (35 x 33) = 20 (cm)
   The height is 20 cm.
6. Capacity: 5 x 23.1 = 115.5 (L)
   Volume: 115.5 x 1000 = 115 500 (cm³)
   The capacity of the aquarium is 115.5 L and the volume is 115 500 cm³.
7. Volume of the rock: (92.48 – 73.55) x 1000 = 18 930 (cm³)
   The volume of the rock was 18 930 cm³.
8. Volume of the water:
   42 x 30 x 38 = 47 880 (cm³) = 47.88 (L)
   It contains 47.88 L of water.

p.40 Capacity

1. A: 5.4 L   B: 5.25 L   C: 5 L
2. Group A
3. 5.25 + 0.35 x 5 = 7
   She buys 7 L of juice in all.
4. 18 x 18 x 18 = 5832 (cm³) = 5.832 (L)
   The capacity of the cube is 5.832 L, which can hold more than 5 L. So, it will not overflow.
5. 1000 ÷ 5 = 200 ; 200 C can fill a 1-m³ box.

p.41 Unit Conversions

1. t ; mg
2. t
3. g
4. mg
5. kg
6. 2.98 ; 2 980 000
7. 46 900 ; 0.0469
8. 0.408 ; 408 000
9. 53 000 ; 0.053
10. 26 000 000 ; 26

p.42 Mass

1. 504 ÷ 36 = 14 (g) ; Each cookie weighs 14 g.
2. 14 x 20 = 280 (g) ; 20 cookies weigh 280 g or 0.28 kg.
3. The cake weighs: 2.2 – 0.504 = 1.696 (kg)
   The cake weighs 1.696 kg.
4. 1.696 ÷ 8 = 0.212 (kg) ;
   Each slice weighs 0.212 kg or 212 g.

p.43 Mass

1. 0.326 ; 326 000
2. 52 ; 0.052
3. 0.00115 ; 1150
4. 52 kg
5. 1000
6. 115 t
7. 230 g
8. 0.13 kg

p.46 Angles

1. A: acute ; 35°   B: right angle ; 90°
   C: obtuse angle ; 122°   D: reflex angle ; 305°
   E: acute angle ; 40°   F: straight angle ; 180°
   G: obtuse angle ; 143°
2. 2

p.47 Constructing Figures

1.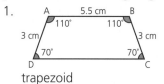
trapezoid

2.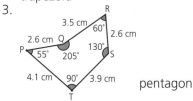
parallelogram

3.
pentagon

p.48 Drawing 3-D Models

1. 2. 3.
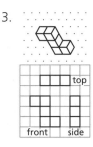

p.49 Combined Transformations

1. A: (2,7), (2,4), (4,5)   B: (8,1), (11,1), (11,3)
   C: (15,2), (18,2), (18,5), (16,5)
2.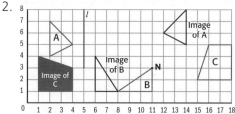

(Suggested answer)

3. Rotate C a $\frac{1}{4}$ turn clockwise about (16,5). Then translate it 12 squares left and 2 squares down.

p.50 Congruent Figures

1. $\angle A = 31°$; $\angle B = 110°$; $\angle C = 39°$;
$\angle P = 31°$; $\angle Q = 110°$; $\angle R = 39°$;
AB = 6 cm ; BC = 5 cm ; CA = 9.1 cm ;
PQ = 6 cm ; QR = 5 cm ; RP = 9.1 cm ; congruent

2.

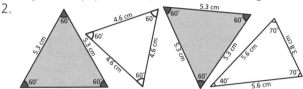

p.51 Similar Figures

1. equal ; equal ; similar
2. Colour A and F with the same colour and B and E with another colour.
3. Colour P and S with the same colour.

p.52 Rotational Symmetry

1. A: No ; 0   B: Yes ; 3
   C: Yes ; 2   D: Yes ; 4
2. (Suggested answers)

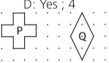

p.53 Tiling Patterns

1.

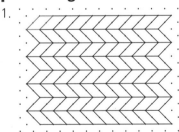

2. (Individual answers)

p.56 Equations

1. A ; 9   2. B ; 15
(Suggested symbols for questions 3 and 4)
3. y ; $3 \times y = 12$; $y = 4$; The cost of a box is $4.
4. a = the number of children ;
   $16 \div a = 2$; $a = 8$; There are 8 children.

p.57 Number Patterns

1a. + 24 ; + 72 ; + 216 ; + 648
 b. triples ; × 3
 c. 5 ; Multiply by 3, and then subtract 2 each time. ;
    26 245
2a. − 1024 ; − 512 ; − 256 ; − 128 ; − 64
 b. one half ; ÷ 2

c. 2054 ; Divide by 2, and then add 3 each time. ; 14

p.58 Number Patterns

1. B ; 186 ; 378   2. C ; 165 ; 489
3. A ; 47 ; 95   4. D ; 742 ; 1478
5. E ; 648 ; 972
6. 13 ; 17 ; 21 ; 25 ;
   Start at 5. Add 2 each time. ;
   Start at 13. Add 4 each time. ; 23 ; 49
7. 24 ; 27 ; 30 ; 33 ;
   Start at 12. Add 1 each time. ;
   Start at 24. Add 3 each time. ; 21 ; 51

p.59 Solve Problems Using Patterns

1. 83 ; 163 ; 323
2. Start at 8. Multiply by 2, and then subtract 3 each time.
3. 1283 marbles
4. 386 ; 194 ; 98 ; 50 ; 26 ; 14 ; 8
5. Start at 386. Divide by 2, and then add 1 each time.
6. Box 8

p.60 Number Patterns

1.

Input	Output	(Input,Output)
2	4	(2,4)
4	10	(4,10)
6	16	(6,16)
8	22	(8,22)
10	28	(10,28)

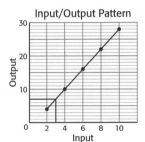

output number: 7

2.

Input	Output	(Input,Output)
10	6	(10,6)
20	11	(20,11)
30	16	(30,16)
40	21	(40,21)
50	26	(50,26)

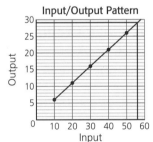

input number: 56

P.61 Geometric Patterns

1.   2.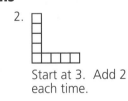

Start at 25. Subtract 1. Increase the number you subtract by 2 each time.

Start at 3. Add 2 each time.

p.62-63 Geometric Patterns

1.

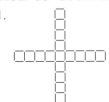

Answers

2.

Frame	No. of ☐	No. of / Used	Perimeter (cm)
1	1	4	4
2	5	16	12
3	9	28	20
4	13	40	28
5	17	52	36

3. Multiply the number of squares by 2, and then add 2 to get the perimeter.
4. Multiply the number of squares by 3, and then add 1 to get the number of sticks used.
5. The number of sticks used is 88 and the perimeter is 60 cm.
6. Ordered Pair: (2,12) ; (3,20) ; (4,28) ; (5,36)

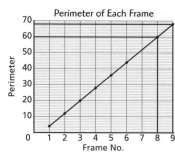

Perimeter of Each Frame

7a. 60   b. Frame 9

p.66-67 Mean, Median, Mode

1. 5 m, 10 m, 12 m, 15 m, 40 m, 40 m, 52 m, 55 m, 86 m
2. Mean: $315 \div 9$; 35 (m) ; Median: 40 m ; Mode: 40 m
3. The new mean will be greater because the height of the new tower is greater than the old mean.
4. 33 m ; 27.5 m ; 15 m, 40 m
5. 32.5 m ; 27.5 m ; 40 m

p.68 Circle Graph

1. Angle of Measure: 90° ; 120° ; 90° ; 60° ;
   Fraction: $\frac{1}{4}$; $\frac{1}{3}$; $\frac{1}{4}$; $\frac{1}{6}$
2. green   3. $\frac{1}{2}$
4. Any colour other than yellow, green, or blue.
5. 20 children   6. 25 children

p.69 Coordinates

1. A: (4,5)   B: (4,6)   C: (6,4)   D: (4,2)
   E: (4,3)   F: (1,3)   G: (1,5)
2. P(12,5), Q(12,6), R(10,4), S(12,2), T(12,3), U(15,3), V(15,5)
3.

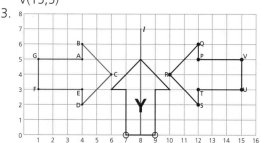

p.70 Scatter Plot

1. A ; D
2. A ; a downward ; The number of items sold decreases as the price increases.
3. Yes. It shows an upward trend. The more time spent on studying, the higher the Math scores.

p.71 Probability

1a. 0.15, $\frac{3}{20}$, 15%   b. 0.4, $\frac{8}{20}$, 40%
  c. 0, 0, 0
2a. 0.2, $\frac{10}{50}$, 20%   b. 0.3, $\frac{15}{50}$, 30%
  c. 0.5, $\frac{25}{50}$, 50%   d. 1, $\frac{50}{50}$, 100%

p.72 Experimental and Theoretical Probabilities

1. $\frac{1}{6}$; $\frac{1}{6}$; $\frac{1}{6}$; $\frac{1}{6}$; $\frac{1}{6}$; $\frac{1}{6}$
2a. $\frac{4}{30}$; $\frac{5}{30}$; $\frac{5}{30}$; $\frac{4}{30}$; $\frac{6}{30}$; $\frac{6}{30}$
  b. $\frac{2}{30}$; $\frac{7}{30}$; $\frac{6}{30}$; $\frac{3}{30}$; $\frac{2}{30}$; $\frac{10}{30}$

p.73 Tree Diagram

1.

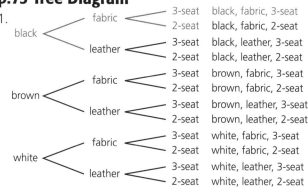

2a. $\frac{1}{12}$ b. $\frac{6}{12}$ c. $\frac{3}{12}$ d. $\frac{4}{12}$